Young Learner's

Look-n-Colour FRUITS AND VEGETABLES

FRUITS

APPLE

GRAPEFRUIT

GRAPES

PEAR

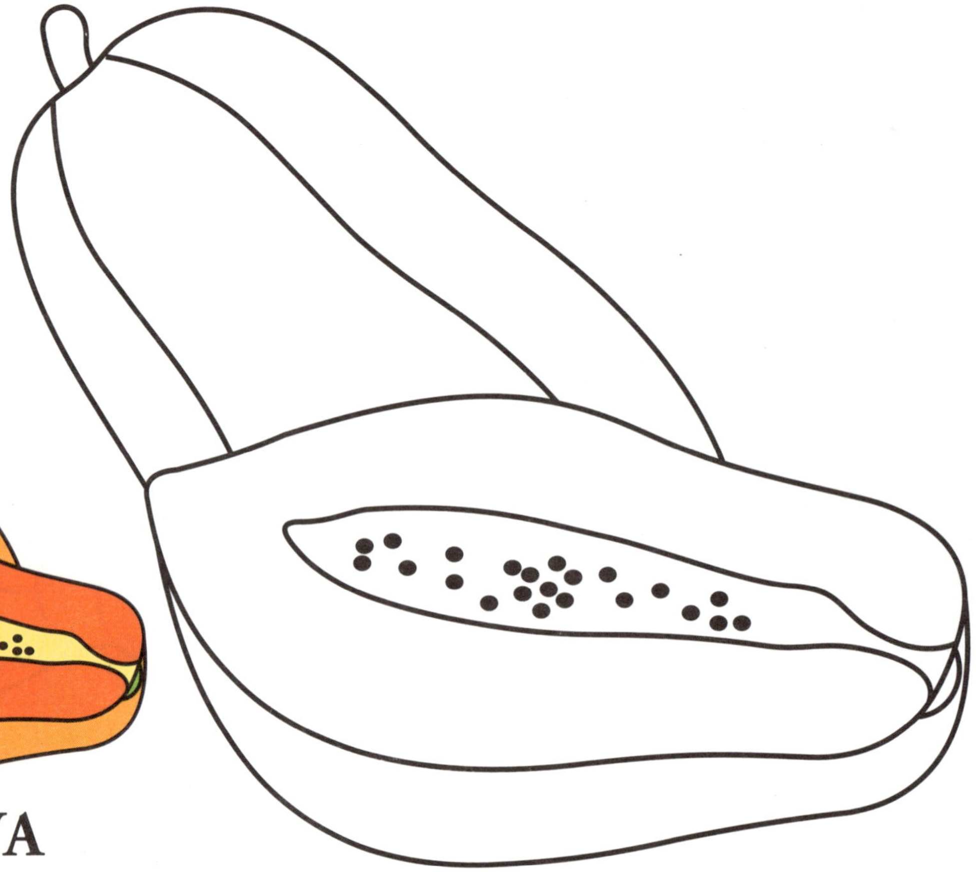

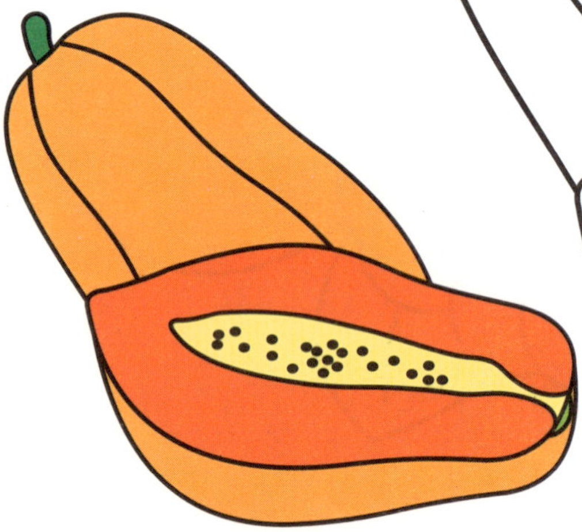

PAPAYA

KIWI

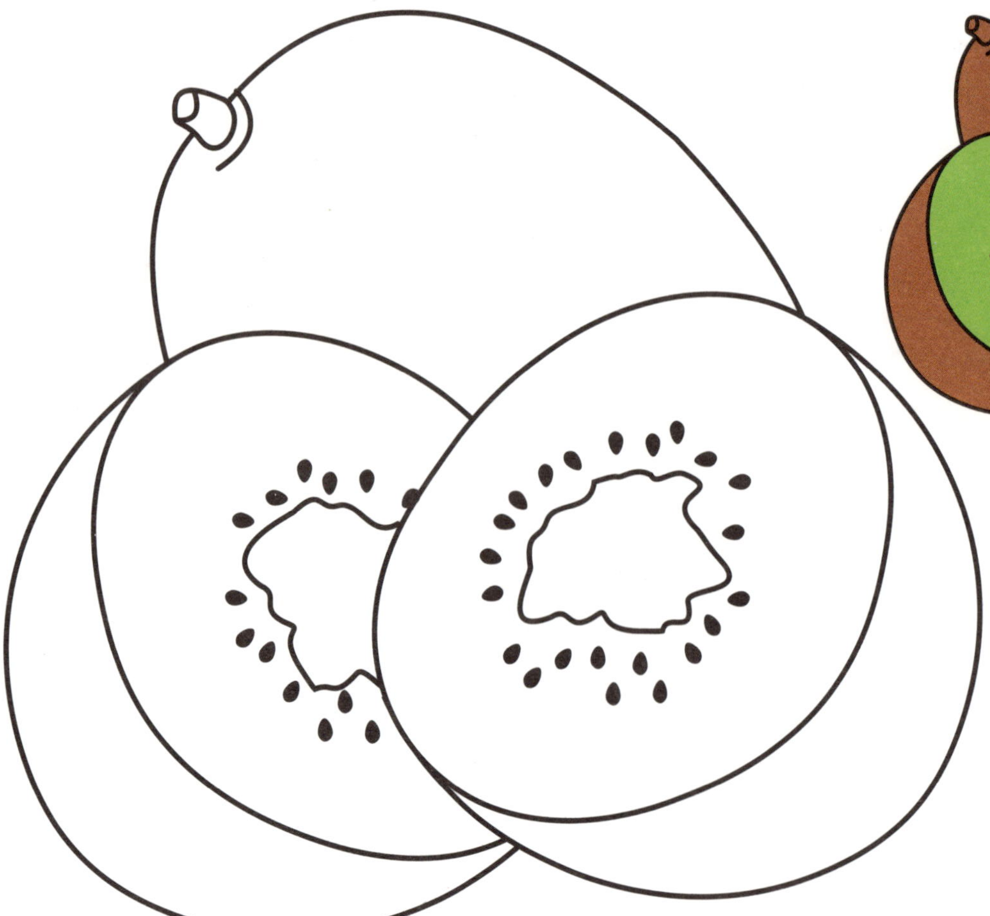

PEACH

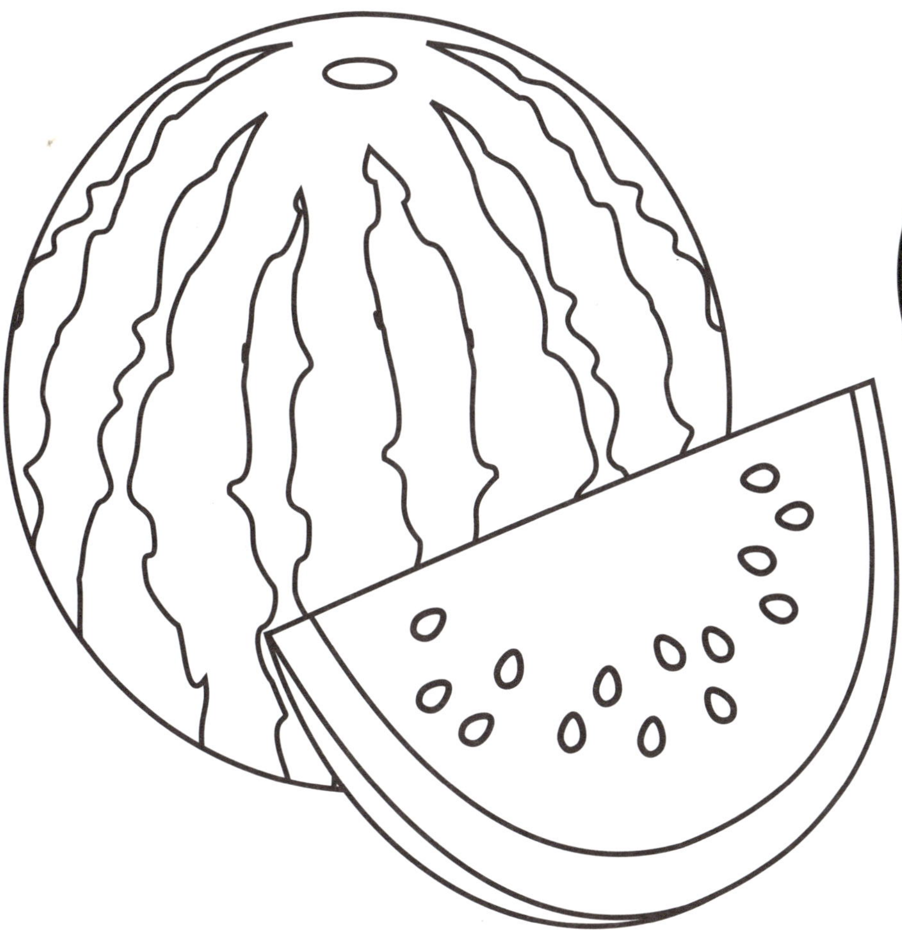

WATERMELON

MANGO

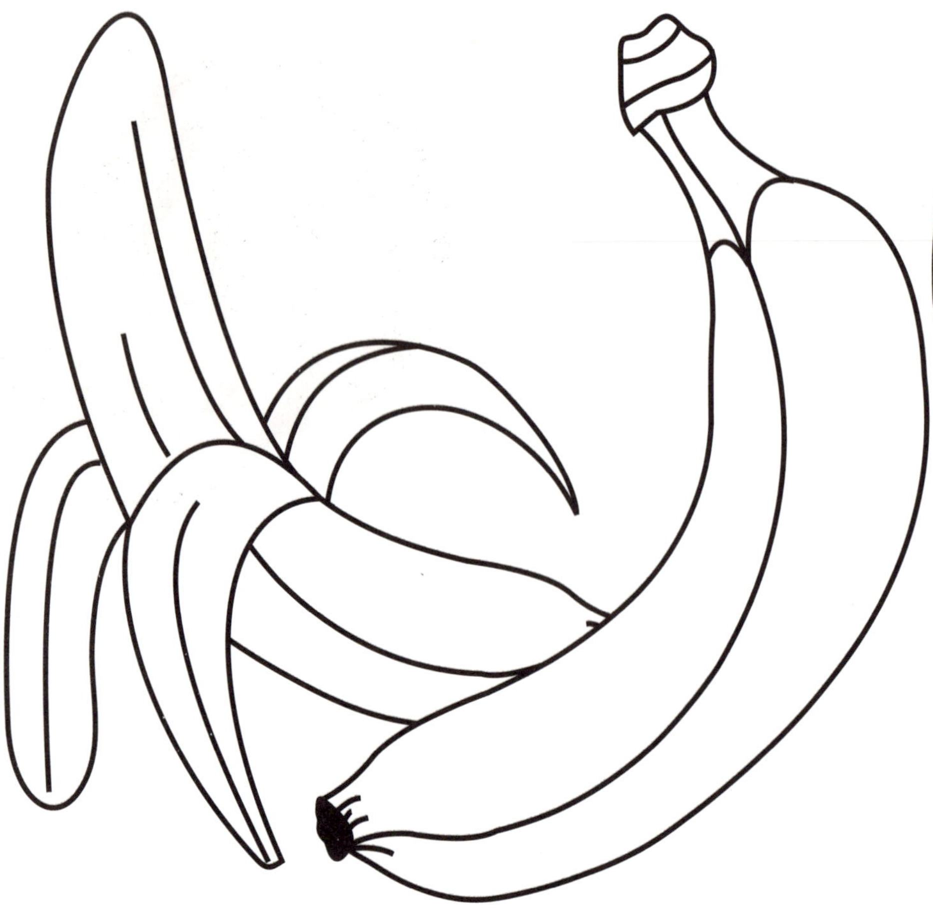

BANANA

ORANGE

STRAWBERRY

MUSKMELON

DRAGON FRUIT

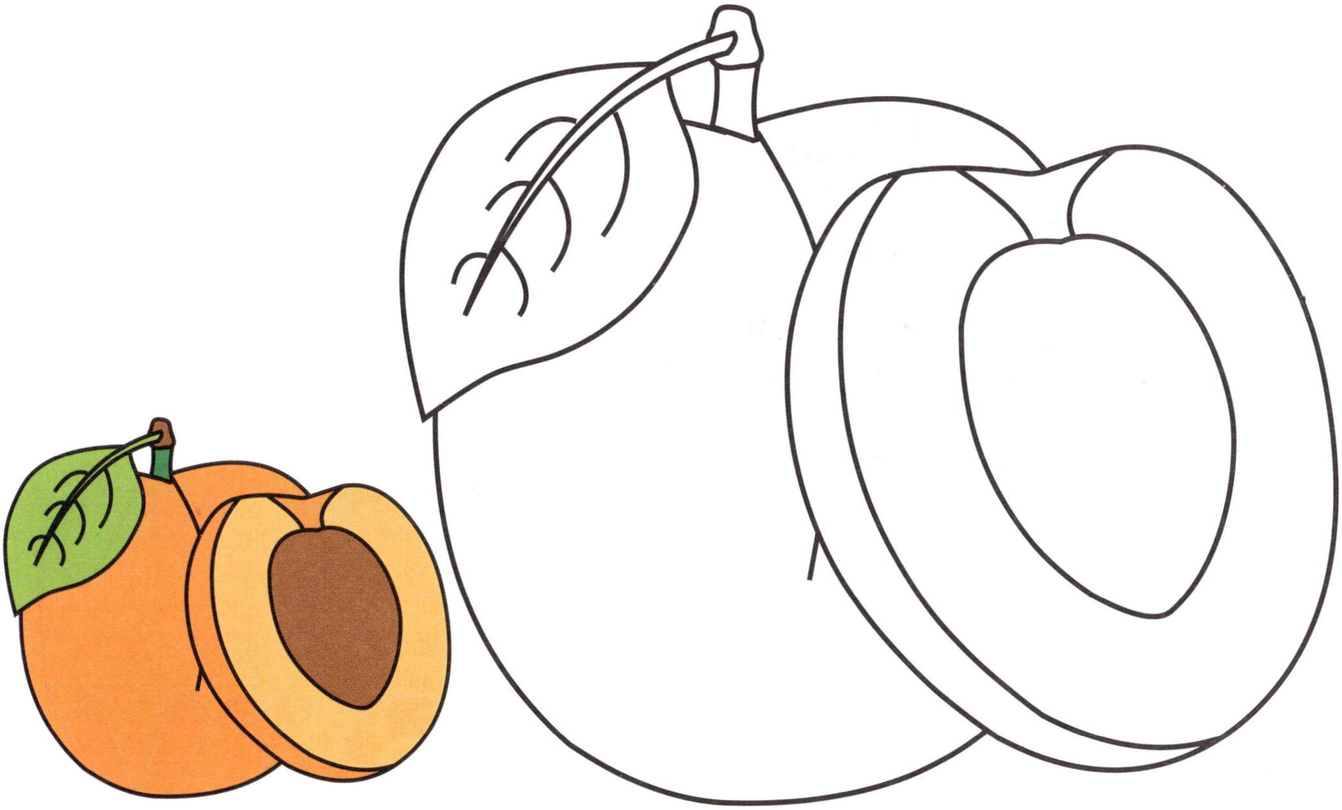

APRICOT

PASSION FRUIT

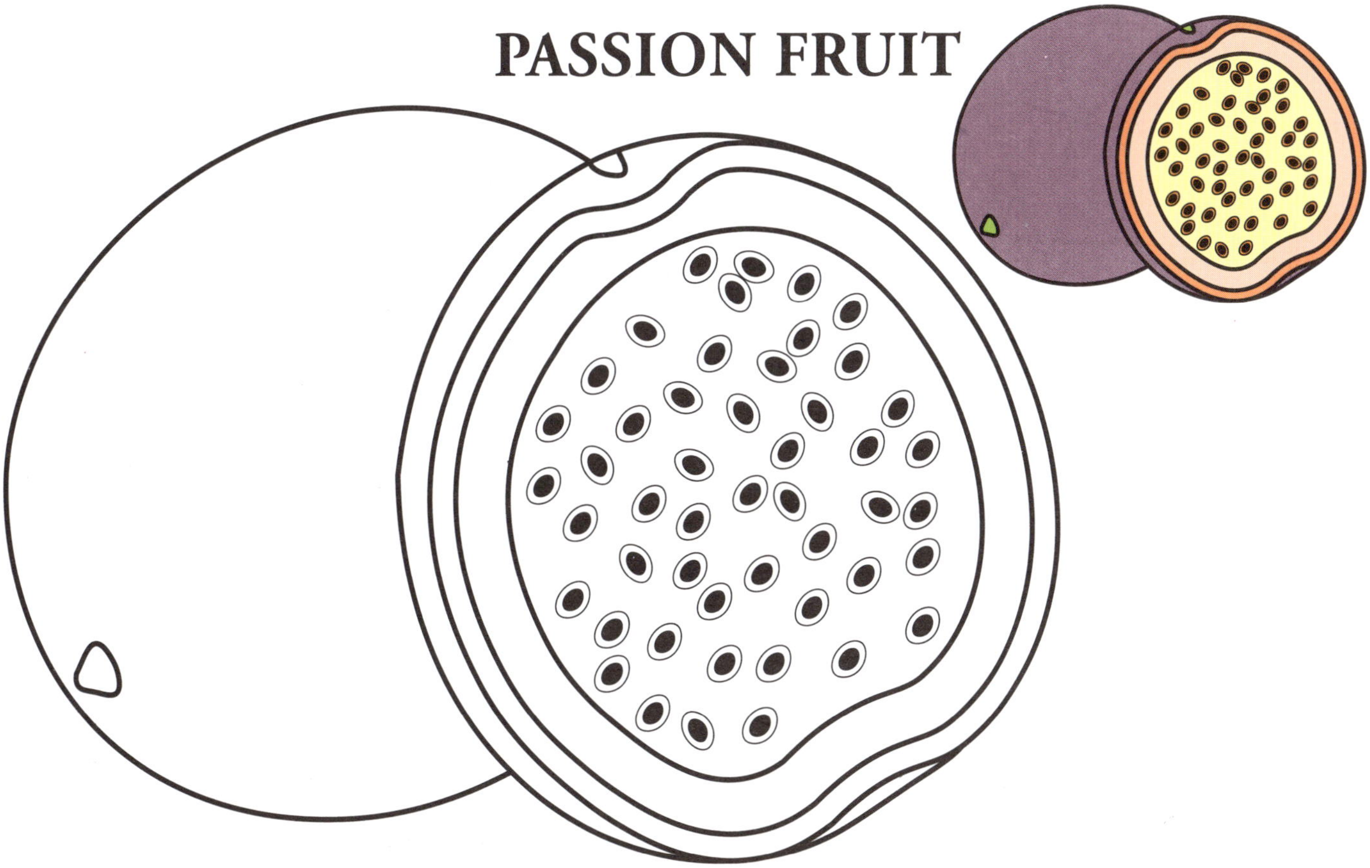

GUAVA

CHERRY

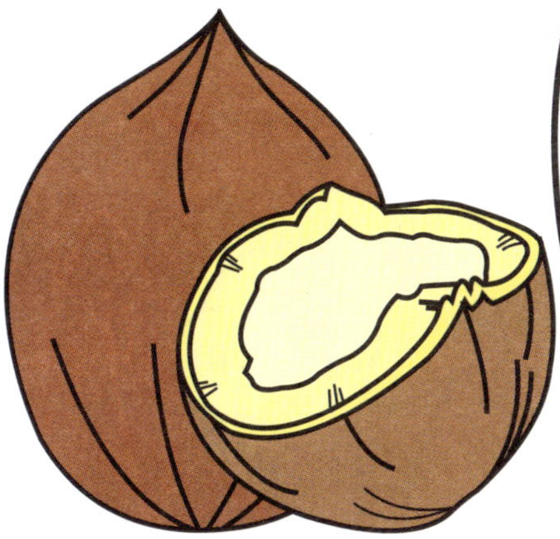

COCONUT

NECTARINE

RASPBERRY

PLUM

VEGETABLES

POTATO

CAPSICUM

CAULIFLOWER

BROCCOLI

EGGPLANT

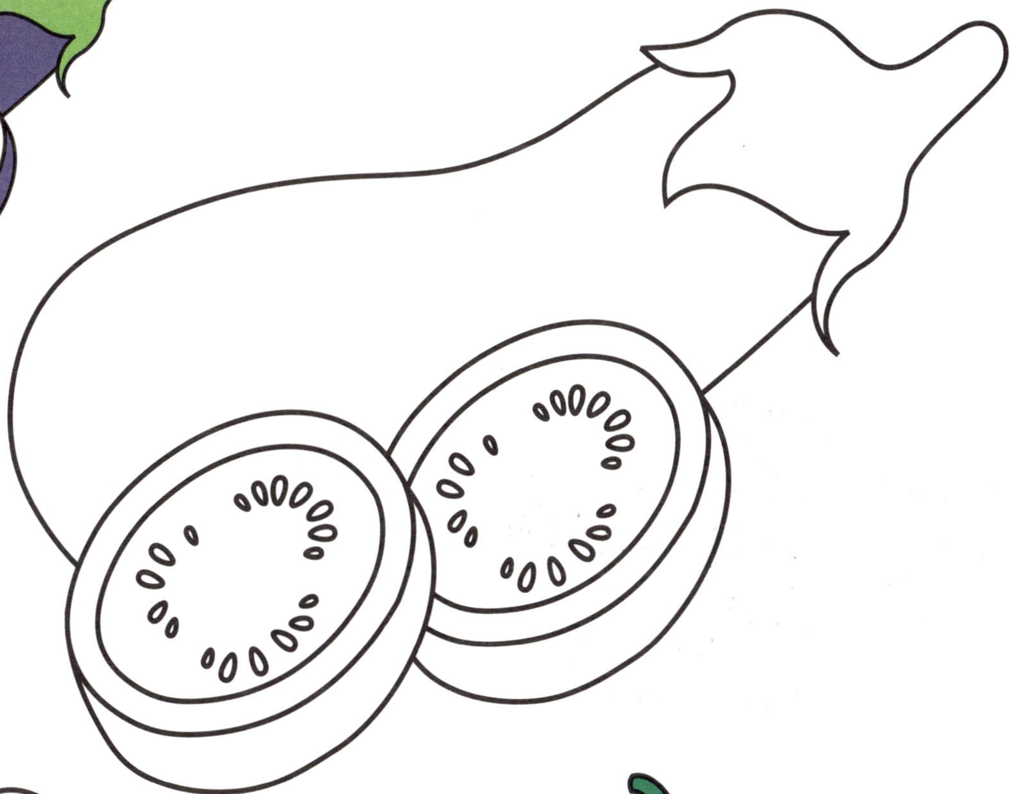

PUMPKIN

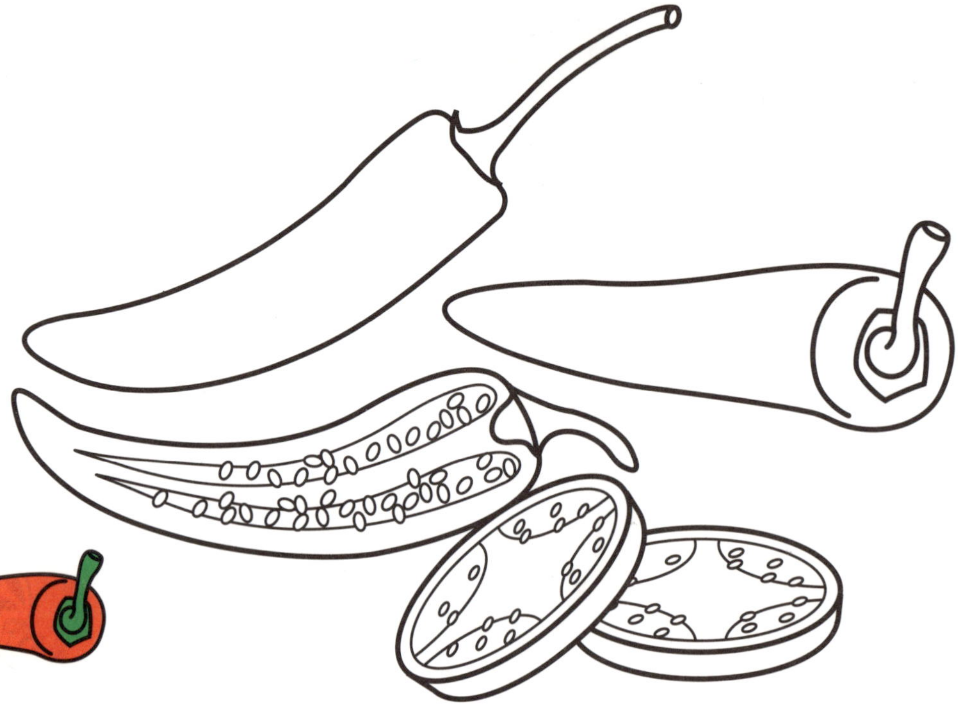

CHILLY

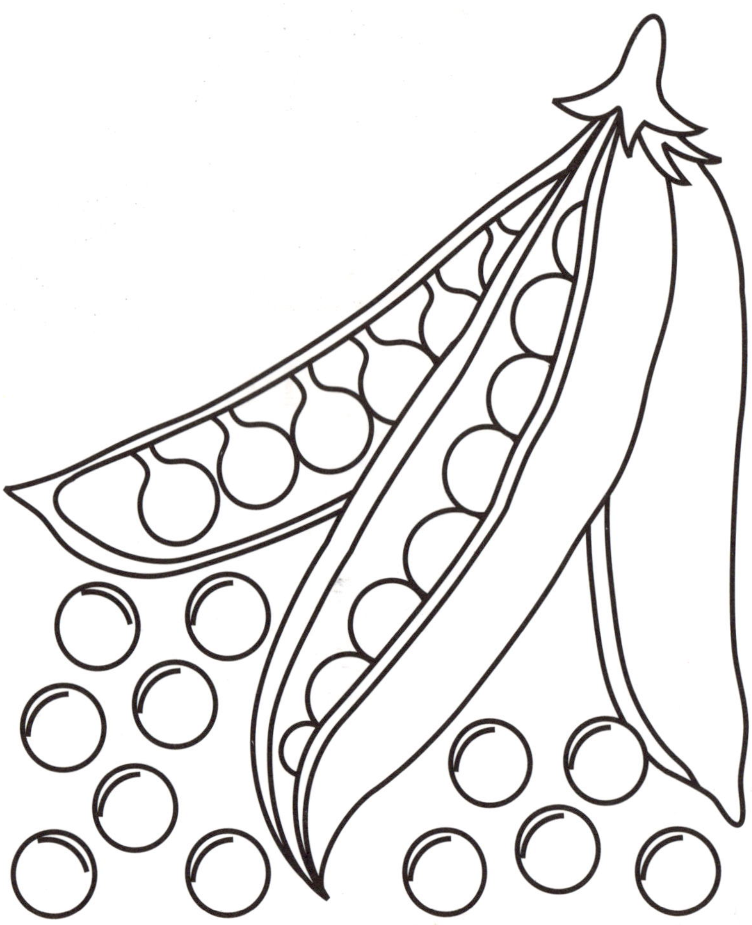

PEAS

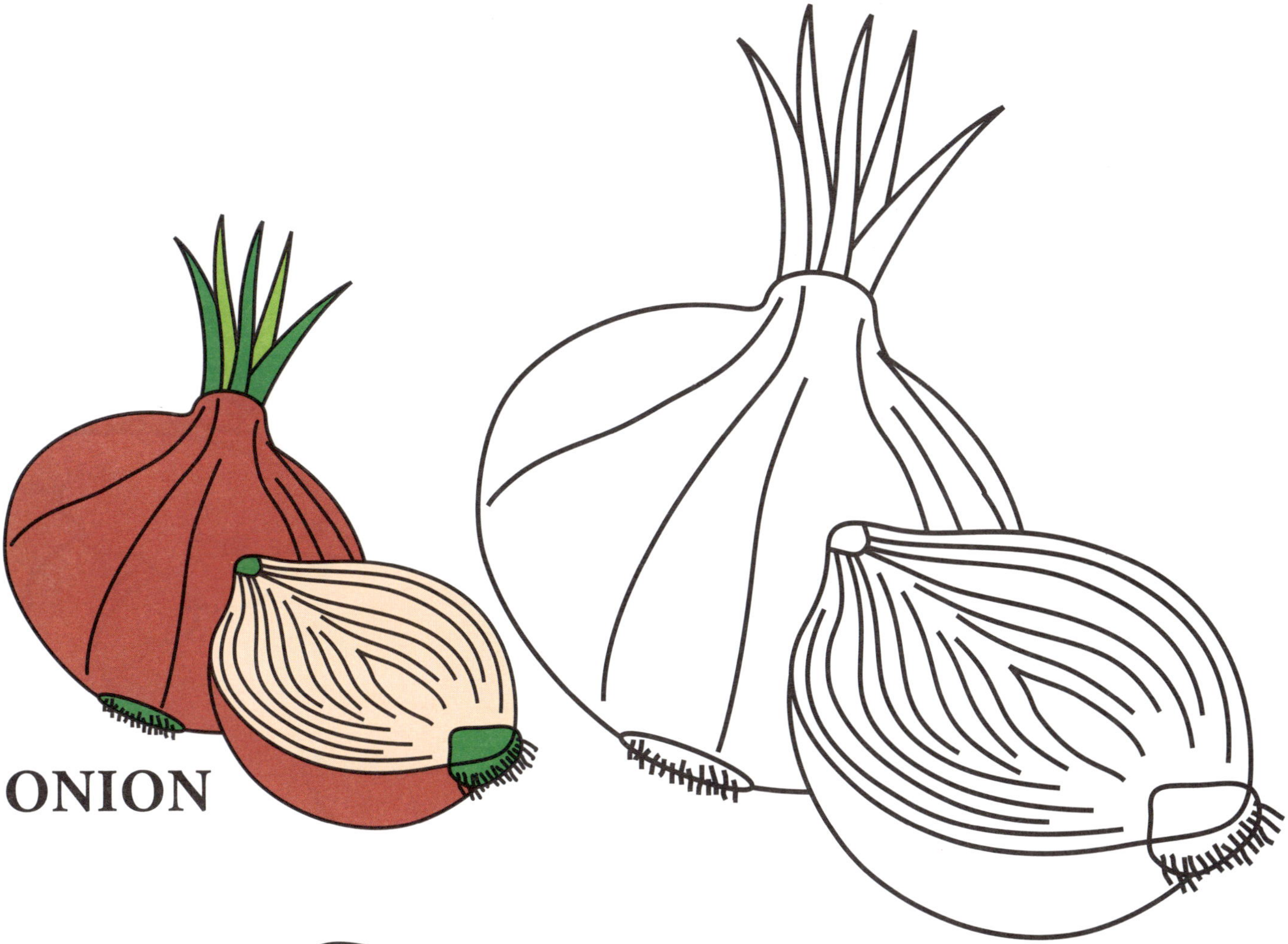

ONION

CABBAGE

BEETROOT

MUSHROOM

CARROT

TURNIP

KOHLRABI

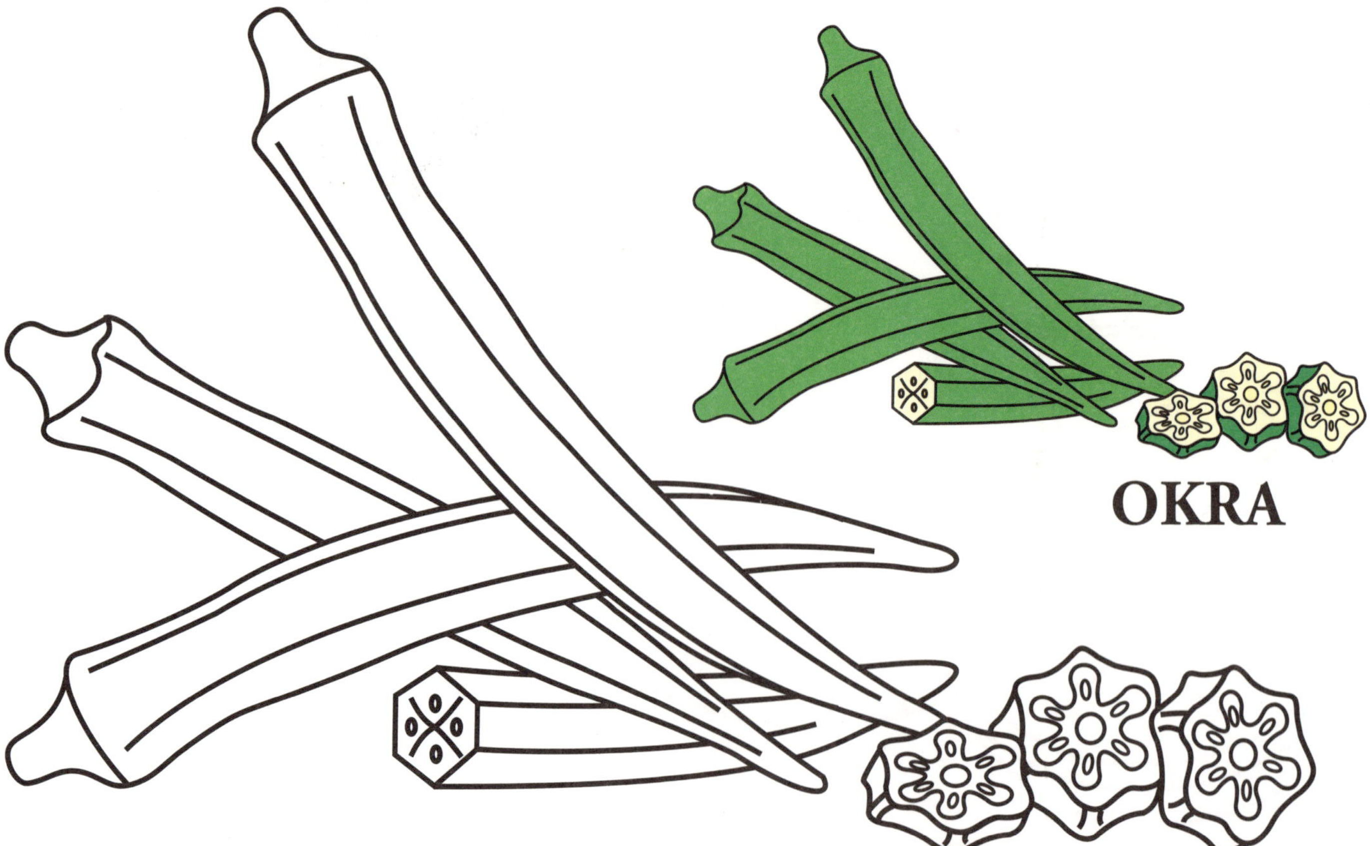

OKRA

BITTER GOURD

BOTTLE GOURD

GARLIC

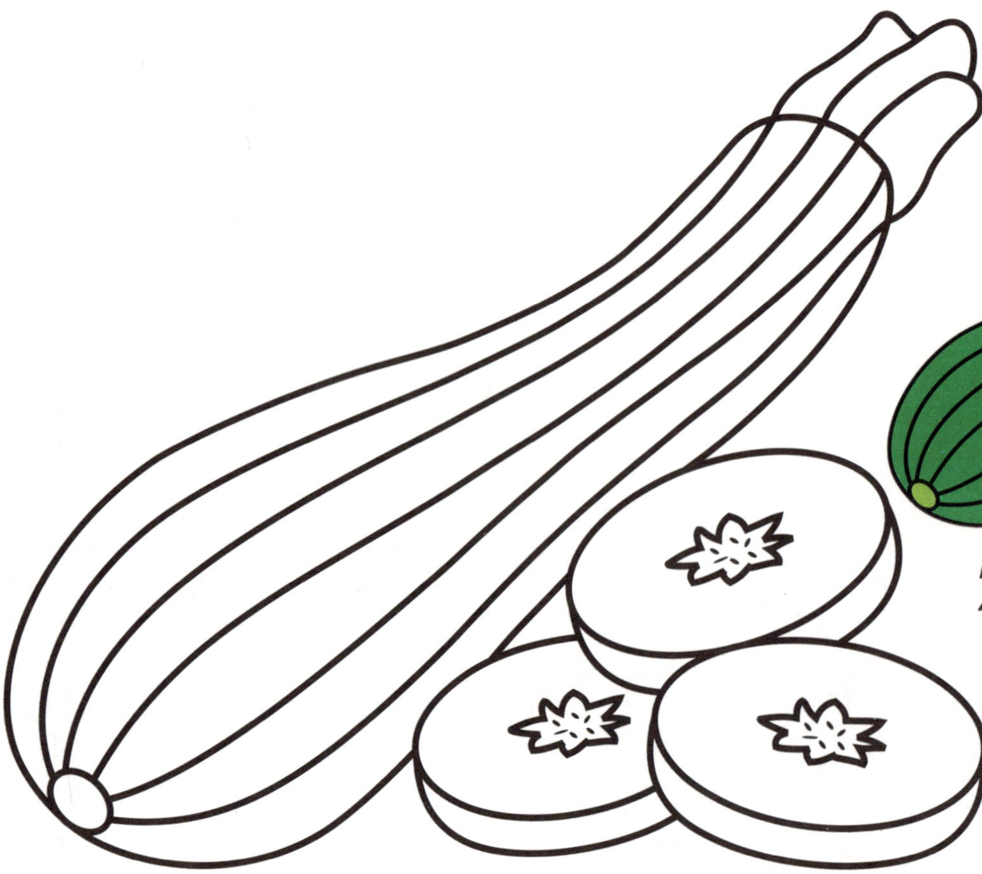

ZUCCHINI

FENUGREEK LEAVES

YAM

ARTICHOKE

SPINACH LEAVES